Figure Weights Practice Book

Improve

WISC®-V

Test-Taking Skills

With 100 Exercises

Zoe Hampton

Published by Perfect Consulting B.V.

Other IQ books by the author

https://prfc.nl/go/amznbooks

Our Mobile Applications for IQ Training

https://prfc.nl/go/allapps

Follow us on social media

Web site: https://prfc.nl/go/pc

Facebook: https://prfc.nl/go/fbpc

Instagram: https://prfc.nl/go/inpc

LinkedIn: https://prfc.nl/go/lipc

YouTube: https://prfc.nl/go/ytpc

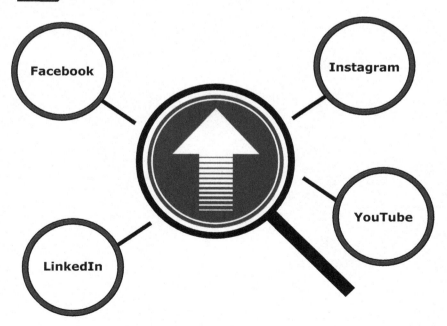

Table of Contents

Introduction

WISC®-V Test
Figure Weights Practice Book

The Weschler Intelligence Scale for Children/WISC® is used to assess intelligence in children aged 6 to 16. It consists of 16 primary and five complementary sub-tests. The WISC®-V assessment takes between 50 and 65 minutes to complete. The purpose of the test is to determine whether or not the child is gifted, as well as the student's cognitive strengths and weaknesses.

About this book

This practice book consists 100 Figure Weights exercises (suitable for children aged 6 to 16), subtest instructions and answer key with detailed explanations. These exercises will help you improve your WISC®-V test-taking skills.

Figure Weights is a new subtest of the WISC®-V. Figure Weights is a Fluid Reasoning subtest that assesses both quantitative and inductive fluid reasoning. Within this practice book are 100 questions from this subtest. Working within a time limit, the child examines one or two scales balanced by weights and a scale with missing weights, and then selects the weights that keep the scale balanced from the answer options.

During the real test, the child must answer the questions within a certain time. The questions start with easier ones and gradually become more difficult. Success!

Instructions:
Show the scales to the child and explain that each figure represents a weight. The child must select an answer to balance the weights in the empty scale.

Exercises with ONE scale

Figure Weights

1

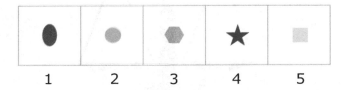

| 1 | 2 | 3 | 4 | 5 |

2

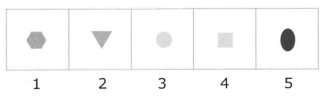

| 1 | 2 | 3 | 4 | 5 |

1	2	3	4	5

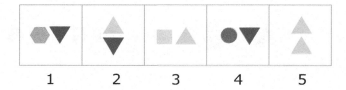

1	2	3	4	5

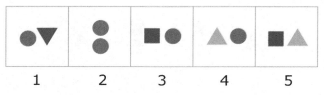

5

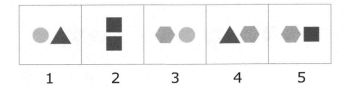

| 1 | 2 | 3 | 4 | 5 |

6

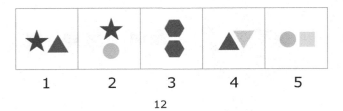

| 1 | 2 | 3 | 4 | 5 |

13

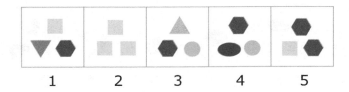

      1   2   3   4   5

      1   2   3   4   5

Exercises with TWO scales

Figure Weights

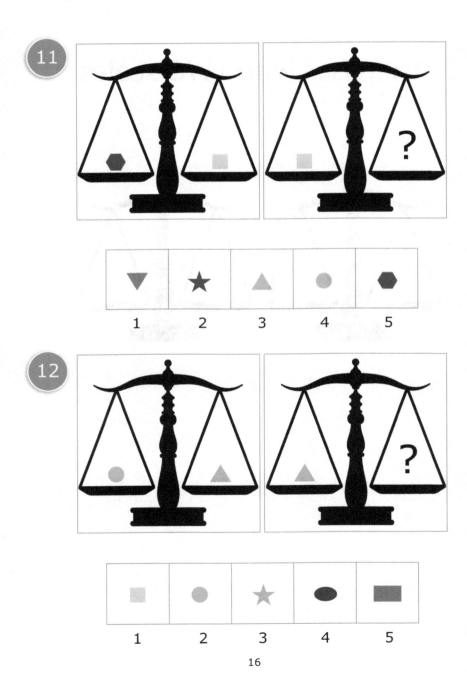

Figure Weights

13

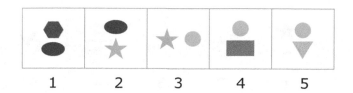

1   2   3   4   5

14

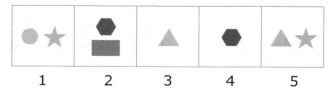

1   2   3   4   5

Figure Weights

15

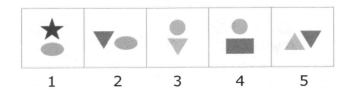

| 1 | 2 | 3 | 4 | 5 |

16

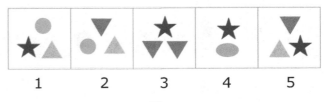

| 1 | 2 | 3 | 4 | 5 |

Figure Weights

17

| 1 | 2 | 3 | 4 | 5 |

18

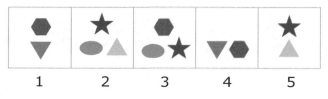

| 1 | 2 | 3 | 4 | 5 |

Figure Weights

19

| 1 | 2 | 3 | 4 | 5 |

20

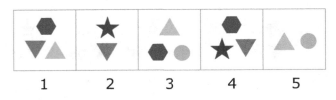

| 1 | 2 | 3 | 4 | 5 |

20

Figure Weights

21

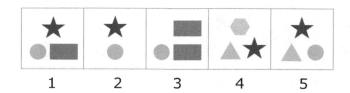

1   2   3   4   5

22

1   2   3   4   5

23

     1   2   3   4   5

24

     1   2   3   4   5

25

1   2   3   4   5

26

1   2   3   4   5

27

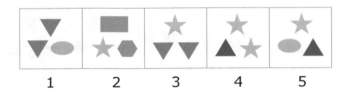

28

24

29

30

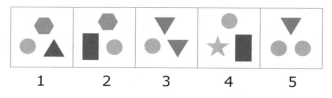

25

31

| 1 | 2 | 3 | 4 | 5 |

32

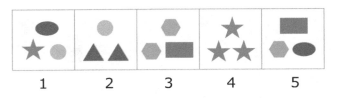

| 1 | 2 | 3 | 4 | 5 |

26

1   2   3   4   5

1   2   3   4   5

Figure Weights

35

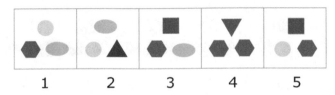

| 1 | 2 | 3 | 4 | 5 |

36

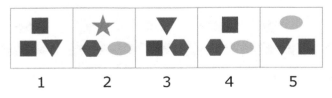

| 1 | 2 | 3 | 4 | 5 |

37

38

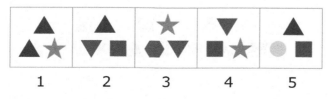

Figure Weights

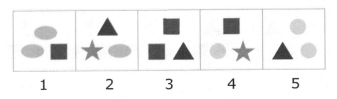

Figure Weights

41

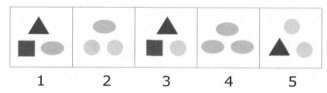

1   2   3   4   5

42

1   2   3   4   5

Figure Weights

43

| 1 | 2 | 3 | 4 | 5 |

44

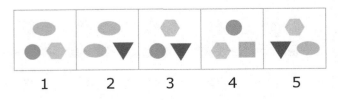

| 1 | 2 | 3 | 4 | 5 |

Figure Weights

45

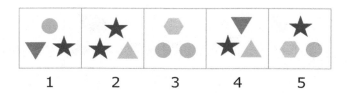

| 1 | 2 | 3 | 4 | 5 |

46

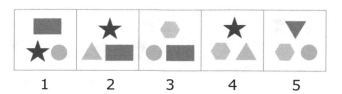

| 1 | 2 | 3 | 4 | 5 |

47

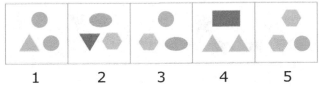

| 1 | 2 | 3 | 4 | 5 |

48

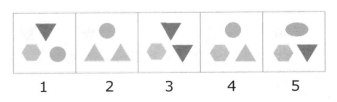

| 1 | 2 | 3 | 4 | 5 |

Figure Weights

49

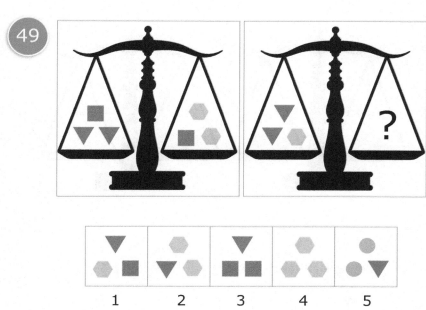

50

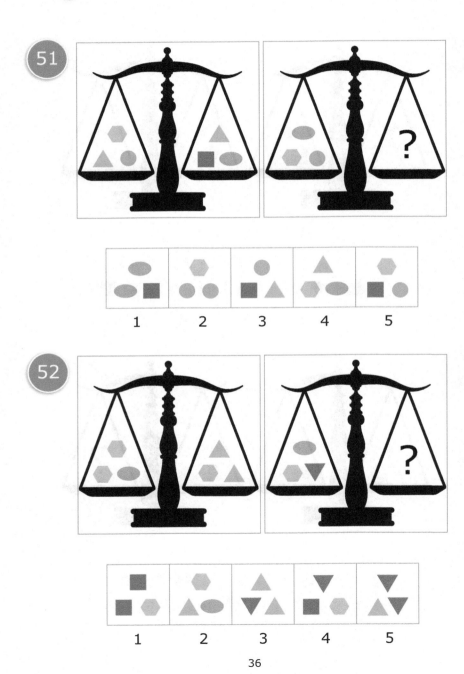

53

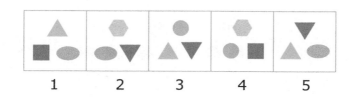

| 1 | 2 | 3 | 4 | 5 |

54

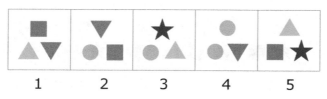

| 1 | 2 | 3 | 4 | 5 |

55

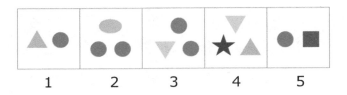

| 1 | 2 | 3 | 4 | 5 |

56

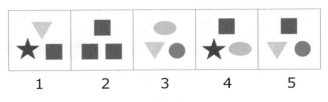

| 1 | 2 | 3 | 4 | 5 |

1   2   3   4   5

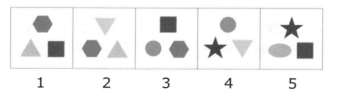

1   2   3   4   5

59

| 1 | 2 | 3 | 4 | 5 |

60

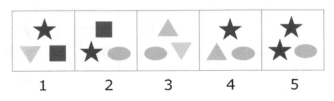

| 1 | 2 | 3 | 4 | 5 |

Exercises with THREE scales

Figure Weights

61

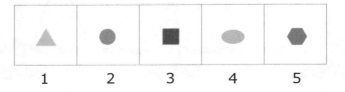

| 1 | 2 | 3 | 4 | 5 |

62

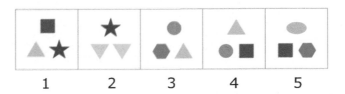

| 1 | 2 | 3 | 4 | 5 |

Figure Weights

63

| 1 | 2 | 3 | 4 | 5 |

64

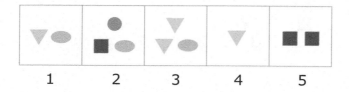

| 1 | 2 | 3 | 4 | 5 |

43

Figure Weights

65

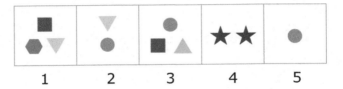

| 1 | 2 | 3 | 4 | 5 |

66

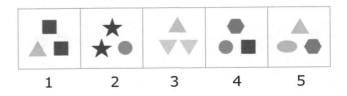

| 1 | 2 | 3 | 4 | 5 |

67

1   2   3   4   5

68

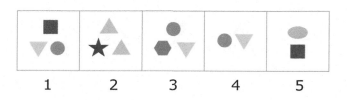

1   2   3   4   5

69

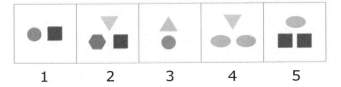

| 1 | 2 | 3 | 4 | 5 |

70

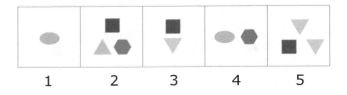

| 1 | 2 | 3 | 4 | 5 |

46

71

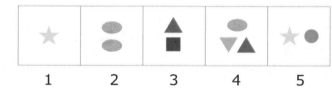

1   2   3   4   5

72

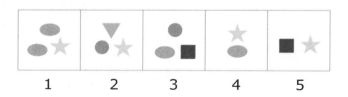

1   2   3   4   5

73

| 1 | 2 | 3 | 4 | 5 |

74

| 1 | 2 | 3 | 4 | 5 |

75

1   2   3   4   5

76

1   2   3   4   5

Figure Weights

77

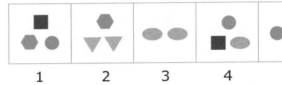

1   2   3   4   5

78

1   2   3   4   5

Figure Weights

79

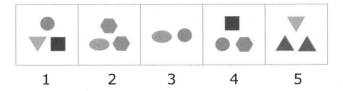

1   2   3   4   5

80

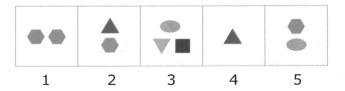

1   2   3   4   5

Figure Weights

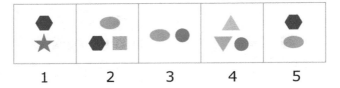

| 1 | 2 | 3 | 4 | 5 |

| 1 | 2 | 3 | 4 | 5 |

52

Figure Weights

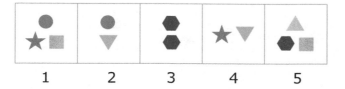

1   2   3   4   5

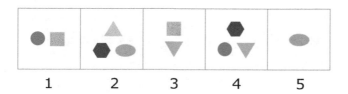

1   2   3   4   5

Figure Weights

85

1	2	3	4	5

86

1	2	3	4	5

Figure Weights

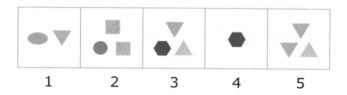

| 1 | 2 | 3 | 4 | 5 |

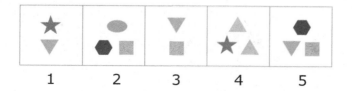

| 1 | 2 | 3 | 4 | 5 |

89

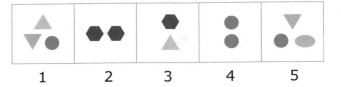

1   2   3   4   5

90

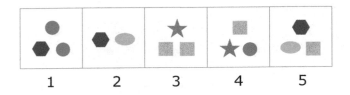

1   2   3   4   5

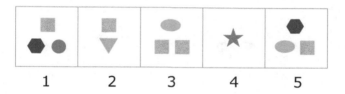

1   2   3   4   5

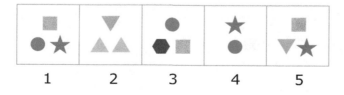

1   2   3   4   5

Figure Weights

93

1   2   3   4   5

94

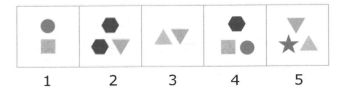

1   2   3   4   5

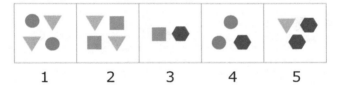

97

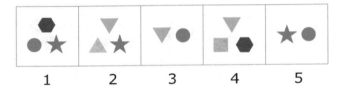

98

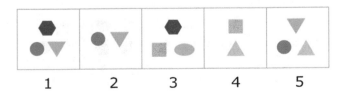

1   2   3   4   5

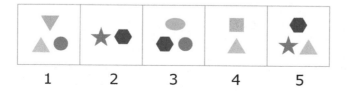

1   2   3   4   5

Answers

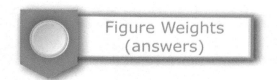

Balance on a scale is achieved when the two sides of the scale have objects of equal weight.

=   The sign represents equality, indicating that the weight on either side is identical.

=> The sign represents a logical consequence, indicating that if the statement on the left is true, then the statement on the right logically follows.

/ When there are two objects of equal weight/type on both sides of the scales they can be removed (but necessarily on both sides)

/ If placed on one side, it must also be placed on the other side.

1.Answer 2   ● = ●

2.Answer 5   ● = ●

3.Answer 2   ▲▼ = ▼▲

4.Answer 3   ■● = ■●

5.Answer 5   ■● = ●■

6.Answer 2   ●★ = ●★

7.Answer 1 ▢●● = ●▢●

8.Answer 3 ●▲★ = ▲●★

9.Answer 1 ●▼▢ = ▼▢●

10.Answer 5●●★ = ★●●

63

11. Answer 5 ⬡ = ⬛

12. Answer 2 ● = ▲

13. Answer 5 ●▼ = ▮●

14. Answer 3 ▲⬢ = ⬢★ => ▲ = ★

15. Answer 5 ▲▼ = ★●

16. Answer 1 ▲●★ = ⬛▼

17. Answer 4 ●/● = ★/● => ★● = ●●

18. Answer 1 ★/● = ▲/● => ● = ● => /● = ●/

19. Answer 5 /★ = ●/ => ●★ = ●▼ => ▼● = ●★

20. Answer 4 ●/ = ▲/ => ⬢ = ● => /● = ★/

21. Answer 2 ▮/ = ★/ => ▮ = ★ => ▮/ = ★/

22. Answer 3 /▼ = /● => ●▲ = ▼▼ => ▲★ = ▼★

23. Answer 2 ★/● = /▲ => ★● = ▼▲ => ▲/ = ●/★

24. Answer 4 ●/ = ▮/● => ●▮ = ★● => /● = ★/

25. Answer 5 /● = ●/ => ▲● = ●▼ => ▮● = ▮●

26. Answer 2 /▼ = /⬢ => ●▼ = ●● => /▼ = /●

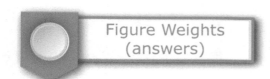
27. Answer 3

28. Answer 4

29. Answer 4

30. Answer 5

31. Answer 1

32. Answer 2

33. Answer 3

34. Answer 1

35. Answer 1

36. Answer 3

37. Answer 5

38. Answer 2

39. Answer 1

40. Answer 4

41. Answer 2

42. Answer 5

43. Answer 4

44. Answer 1

45. Answer 3

46. Answer 2

47. Answer 1

48. Answer 3

49. Answer 4

50. Answer 2

51. Answer 1

52. Answer 3

53. Answer 1

54. Answer 2

55. Answer 5

56. Answer 2

57. Answer 4

58. Answer 3

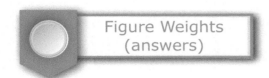
59. Answer 1   ⬆️/◯ = ■/ => ▲◯=■▽ => ■/▽ = ◯/▲

60. Answer 2   ◯/★ = ▽/▲ => ◯★ = ▲▽ => ▲/▽ = ★◯

61. Answer 4   ◯ = ★   and   ★ = ▽   =>   ▽ = ◯

62. Answer 3   ★/◯ = /◯ => ◯⬡ = ◯★ => ★/◯ = ⬡/

63. Answer 5   ▲◯ = ■★ and   ■ = ◯▲ =>   ◯ = ▽★

64. Answer 3   ▽/ = /◯ and   ◯ = ◯ => ◯/ = ▽/▽

65. Answer 5   ▲▽■ = ★◯   and ◯/ = /★⬡ => ■/▽▲ = ◯

66. Answer 3   ★◯/⬡ = ■/★ and ◯◯ = ▽▲ => ■◯ = ▲▽

67. Answer 2   / = ▽/◯ and   ◯ = ★/◯▲ => ⬡/▽ = ★▲

68. Answer 4   ◯/ = ★/▲ and   ▽/◯ = ■⬡ =>★/▲ = ◯▽

69. Answer 5   ▲/■■ = ▽/◯◯ and   ■/▲ = ◯▽ =>   ◯ =■

70. Answer 3   /◯ = ▲// and   /◯ = /■ =>   ◯ =■

71. Answer 2   /▽ = ▲/■/ and   /◯ = ■//▲ =>   ▽ =◯

72. Answer 4   ★/◯◯ = ▲▽ and   /◯ = ▲/ => //■ = /◯★

73. Answer 3   ◯/ = /★◯ and   ◯/★ = ▲/▽★ => ◯★ = ▽★

74. Answer 2   ▲/ = /■◯ and /▲ = / => ■◯ =★

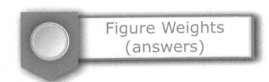

75. Answer 1 ⬡⬢ =⬣⬣ and ⬇⬮ =⬮⬢ => ▲▲ =▼▼

76. Answer 4 ▲⬛ = ⬇⬮ and ▽ = ⬤ => ■▲ =⬤⬤

77. Answer 5 ⬤ = ⬡ and ⬢⬢ =⬇⬛ => ⬛▽⬤ =⬤⬤

78. Answer 2 ⬢⬢ = ▲⬇★ and ★⬮▲=⬢⬢ => ⬤ =▼

79. Answer 1 ⬇⬮⬮ =▲⬮ and ⬤ = ⬡ => ▲ =▼

80. Answer 4 ⬮⬛⬤ = ⬮▽ and ⬇⬮=▲⬛ => ⬤ =▲

81. Answer 3 ⬮★⬤ = ⬛⬮ and ★⬮▽ = ⬤⬛ => ▼ = ⬤

82. Answer 5 ▽▲ =⬤ and ⬮⬤ = ⬮▲ => ⬤▽ =⬤

83. Answer 4 ★▽ =⬢⬤⬛ and ▲⬮=⬢⬢ => ⬛▲⬛ =⬢⬢

84. Answer 2 ⬤▲ = ⬤ and ⬢⬮ =▲⬮ => ⬤ =▲⬤

85. Answer 1 ⬛⬤⬢ = ▲▽ and ▽ = ⬛ => ▲ =⬤

86. Answer 2 ⬮⬮ = ★⬮ and ⬢▽ = ⬤ => ⬤★ =▽⬤⬢

87. Answer 3 ⬛⬮ =⬮⬤ and ⬮⬛ = ⬮▽⬤ => ⬤⬤ =⬢▽

88. Answer 1 ▽⬮ =⬛▲ and ⬢⬢ = ▲⬛ => ⬤⬤ =▽

89. Answer 4 ⬮⬤▽ = ▲⬤⬮ and ⬮▲ = ⬮▽ => ⬤ =⬤

90. Answer 5 ★⬮⬤ = ⬮⬢ and ✳★ = ✳⬤ => ⬤⬤ =⬤⬢

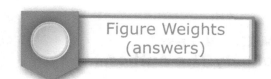

91. Answer 2   ⬟⭐ = ⬟⭐ and ▽ = ● => ● = ▽

92. Answer 5   ⬢△△ = ▽▽ and ● = ●△ => △ = ▽■

93. Answer 5   ◻● = ●● and ▽△ = ● => △▽ = ●●

94. Answer 2   ⭐●▽ = △■● and ▽■ = △● => ⭐ = ●

95. Answer 2   ⬢●● = ⬢■ and ■▱ = ▱● => ▽▽■▱ = ●▱

96. Answer 3   ⬢△ = ●▽ and ■■ = ▽ => ●△ = ●■■

97. Answer 5   ⭐●▱ = ▽⭐ and ⬢△⭐ = ▽ => ▽ = ●   ●=⭐

98. Answer 4   ▽▱⬢ = △▱ and ●△ = ■ => ▽● = ■

99. Answer 5   ⭐▱△ = ▱▽ and ▽● = △△ => △ = ⭐

=> ⭐⭐ = ▽●

100. Answer 2 ■△● = ⭐⭐ and ■▱ = ⭐▱ => ●△ = ⭐

Other WISC-V Test
Practice Books By The Author

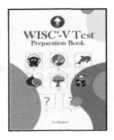

➤ WISC-V Test Preparation Book

https://prfc.nl/go/amwiscvtwo

➤ Practice Book for the WISC-V Test

https://prfc.nl/go/amwiscv

➤ WISC-V Test: New Subtests Practice Book

https://prfc.nl/go/amznbooks

WPPSI-IV Test
Practice Books By The Author

➤ WPPSI™-IV Test: Processing Speed
Practice Book
https://prfc.nl/go/amznbooks

➤ WPPSI™-IV Test: Nonverbal Practice Book
https://prfc.nl/go/amznbooks

Thank you for your purchase!
I hope you enjoyed this book!

Please consider leaving a review!
https://prfc.nl/go/abreview

Made in the USA
Columbia, SC
15 April 2025

56678930R00043